THE MURDER OF MUHASSIN

THE PROPHET'S THIRD GRANDSON

Compiled by

Sheikh al-Habib

The Murder of Muhassin:
The Prophet's Third Grandson

Compiled by Sheikh al-Habib
First Edition

ISBN 978 1 3999 3710 8

The Rafida Foundation
The Minor Land of Fadak
Windmill Road, Fulmer
Buckinghamshire
SL3 6HF

The Rafida Foundation
Charity no. 1182789
rafida.org

INTRODUCTION

In the name of Allah, the Most Beneficent, the Most Merciful

May the ultimate peace and blessings of the Almighty Allah be upon Muhammad and his progeny, the pure, the immaculate; and may His ultimate and continuous wrath befall their enemies.

The martyrdom of the Prophet's third grandson, al-Muhassin son of Ali (peace be upon them both), is a day to remember every year. On this day, we commemorate the tragic death of this stillborn foetus due to the savage attack Umar ibn al-Khattab waged on the house of Sayeda Fatimah al-Zahra (peace be upon her); the only daughter remained after the martyrdom of the holy Prophet of Islam (peace be upon him and his pure family).

It was only five days after Prophet Muhammad (peace be upon him and his pure family) had returned to His lord, when Umar ibn al-Khattab along with an association of malefactors broke into the house to take the legitimate Commander of the Faithfuls, Amir al-Mu'minin Ali ibn Abi Talib (peace be upon him and his father), by means of terror and absolute force to pledge allegiance to the illegitimately appointed Abu Bakr son of Abu Quhafah.

The Day of the attack[1] is considered to be the most grievous, tragic, atrocious and irremediable calamity to ever befall the pure household of the Prophet (peace be upon them). It is in fact more agonising than the day of Ashura on which the Master of Martyrs, al-Hussain son of Ali (peace be upon them both), was brutally slaughtered on the plains of Karbala.

It has been reported that Imam Jaffar al-Saddiq (peace be upon him) had said: "There is no tragedy like ours at Karbala, even though the day of Saqifah[2] and the day on which the door was burnt on Amir al-Mu'minin, Fatimah, al-Hassan, al-Hussain, Zainab, Um Kulthoom and Fidah; on which al-Muhassin was killed by the kick is greater and worse because it is the origin of the Day of Torment[3]."

Therefore, The Day of the attack should be significantly observed and highly commemorated for it was the beginning for all the calamities that afflicted the pure household (peace be upon them) from that time forth. It should be given a great

---

[1] The attack on the house of Lady Fatimah (peace be upon her) is one of the key scenes highlighted in the Lady of Heaven movie; a movie that depicts the historical story of Lady Fatimah (peace be upon her) and her suffering.

[2] The day of Saqifah refers to the day on which a gathering took place at the Saqifah of Bani Sa'ida where Abu Bakr illegitimately seized the commandership of believers after the martyrdom of the holy Prophet (peace be upon upon him and his pure family).

[3] Al-Hidayah al-Kubra by al-Khusaibi.

importance similar to the importance given to the day of Ashura by organising events, ceremonies, Majalis [4] and marches as well as broadcasting adequate media coverage. This will certainly contribute to raising awareness and keeping the tragedy revived in the hearts and minds of the believers as well as it will also conduce to dispelling doubts and strengthening beliefs.

We hereby put in your hands this account known as the "Maqtal" which narrates the martyrdom story of al-Muhassin son of Ali (peace be upon them both) translated into English, by which we seek to encourage the believers to narrate it at the Majalis alongside the Arabic Maqtal for non-Arabic speakers.

We ask Allah the Almighty to bestow success upon our believing brothers and sisters who always endeavour to keep the Majalis of the tragedies of the pure household of the Prophet (peace be upon them) revived and enlivened heeding the words of Imam Jaffar al-Sadiq (peace be upon him) to his companion Bukair ibn Muhammad al-Asdi: "Surely, I love those gatherings [held in our remembrance]! So, enliven our affairs".[5]

---

[4] Majalis is plural for Majlis which means a council or gathering held to commemorate and lament the martyrdom of the infallible Imams (peace be upon them).
[5] Thawab al-Ammal

THE MAQTAL

On the night prior to his martyrdom the seal of the messengers, Muhammad son of Abdullah (peace be upon him and his family), summoned his pure family Ali, Fatimah, Hassan and Hussain (peace be upon them). He then commanded the door to be shut and the women to leave the house apart from Um Salamah, who was made to stand guard at the door making sure no one could draw near.

The Prophet then started to converse privately to the members of his pure family (peace be upon them) for a long time while they weep over his condition, which was deteriorating because of the poisonous dose he had been given by Aisha and Hafsa, at the behest of their fathers, when he fell unconscious during his [late] illness.

After a long time had passed, Ali along with Hassan and Hussain came out and stood at the door. People were [standing] behind the door whilst the Prophet's wives were directing their gaze to Ali and his two sons. Aisha said to Ali: "For what reason the Messenger of Allah made you leave but rather held a closed meeting with his daughter at this time?" Ali (peace be upon him) said: "I have knowledge of what he wanted her for; part of it is about what you, your father and his companion were occupied with, whereof they managed to poison him!", to which Aisha dared not to utter a word out of fear!

Ali, the Commander of the Faithfuls, said: "I did not stay for long until I was called in by Fatimah (peace be upon her). I entered upon the Prophet (peace be upon him and his family) while he was in his last breaths. When I saw him in that condition I cried and could not help myself. He asked: O Ali, what is making you cry?! O my brother, this is not the time to cry, the time for separation has drawn near. I therefore leave you in the trust of Allah. My Lord has chosen me for what he has, but I am verily saddened, grieved and anguished for you and for her – he pointed to Fatimah – to be forsaken after me. The people have agreed to unanimously oppress you. I have left you in Allah's trust, and Allah has accepted this from me. O Ali, I have entrusted Fatimah with matters and enjoined her to recite them to you, so fulfil them, as she is the truthful the veracious".

He then embraced Fatimah to himself, and when he was about to speak to her, he was overtaken by tears and was unable to do so! Fatimah cried heavily and said: "O Messenger of Allah! Your crying has broken my heart and stricken me with sorrow. O the Master of all Prophets, O the trusted one of His Lord and His Messenger; His beloved and His Prophet! Who would be for my children after you? Who would be there for your household? Who would Ali, your brother and the supporter of the religion, have? Who is [to attend] to the revelation of Allah [after you]? Fatimah then cried and fell on the Prophet kissing his face. The Prophet (peace be upon him and his family) then kissed her head and said: "May your father be your sacrifice, O Fatimah!" Upon hearing this Fatimah's weeping became louder. The Prophet (peace be upon him and his family) brought her close to his blessed chest and said: "By Allah, my Lord shall take revenge; He shall become angry for your anger; Woe then woe then woe shall be upon the oppressors".

The Prophet (peace be upon him and his family) then cried and his tears were flowing. The Commander of the Faithfuls – Amir al-Mu'minin (peace be upon him) – said: "Seeing the Prophet cry made me feel as if a part of me was lost [in sadness]! His tears fell like rain until his beard and the sheet that was over him both became wet." The Prophet kept embracing Fatimah so close to him not letting go whilst his head was on my chest, and I was supporting it. Hassan and Hussain were kissing the Prophet's feet and crying at the top of their voices.

Meanwhile, Gabriel, Michael and the nearest angels [to Allah The Most Exalted] were descending from heavens to earth in multitudes; all congregating in the house of the Seal of Prophets; wailing at the seen of the Prophet and his daughter Fatimah (peace be upon them and their pure family) cry. The Commander of the Faithfuls (peace be upon him) said: "When I saw Fatimah weeping, I thought that the heavens and earth are weeping for her".

The Messenger of Allah (peace be upon him and his family) said to his daughter Fatimah: "O daughter, Allah is the One Who remains after me upon you and He is the best to remain. [I swear] by the One Who sent me with truth, the throne of Allah, the angels that surround it, the heavens and earths and whatever is within them have all cried for you. O Fatimah, [I swear] by the One Who sent me with truth I shall stand against your enemies, and against those who usurped your right, cut off the fondness for you and lied about me; They shall indeed become [all] rueful".[6]

He then appealed [to Allah] in prayer: "Cursed is he who oppresses her; Cursed is he who usurps her right; Cursed is he who violates her sanctity; Cursed is he who gives her difficulty and fight her; Cursed is he who burns her door; Cursed is he who oppresses her husband; O Allah I disassociate myself from them and they renounce themselves from me".

He then embraced Fatimah, Ali, Hassan and Hussain close to his chest and said: "O Allah I am at peace with them and with whomever are loyal to them; I guarantee that they shall enter Paradise. I am the

---

[6] Bihar al-Anwar vol. 22

enemy of their enemies, their oppressors and whomever encroaches upon them and turns away from them and from their supporters and at war with them; I guarantee that they shall enter hellfire. O Fatimah [I swear] by Allah I shall only be satisfied if you are satisfied, I shall only be satisfied if you are satisfied, and I shall only be satisfied if you are satisfied (he repeated it thrice). He then turned towards The Commander of the Faithfuls (peace be upon him) and said: "Be informed, O Ali, that I am satisfied with whom my daughter is satisfied with, so are my Lord and His angels".[7]

The family of the house of revelation, (peace be upon them) spent their night crying out in grief and lamenting as the final moments of the holy Prophet (peace be upon him and his family), the poisoned, the oppressed, the martyr, were approaching.

In the forenoon of that day, Monday the 28th of the month of Safar 10 AH, the poison dangerously spread in the body of the Seal of Prophets (peace be upon him and his family). During his last moments, the Prophet placed his sacred head in the lap of his brother and successor Ali son of Abu Talib, Amir al-Mu'minin, (peace be upon him); He brought Ali's ear close to his mouth and started passing on to him the hoarded divine prophecies and knowledge of Prophethood and the reverent secrets of the guardianship of faith. He taught him a thousand

---

[7] Bihar al-Anwar vol. 22

doors of knowledge, each door of which opens a thousand more. Then, the forehead of the Prophet (peace be upon him and his family) secreted and his holy body quivered; his eyes were then closed, his hands drooped, and his immaculate pure soul departed his body and returned to its Lord after it was flown in between the hands of the Commander of the Faithfuls (peace be upon him) and made to pass across his face.[8]

A loud cry of sorrow shook the heavens and earth as the world was caught in grief and anguish for the loss of the Seal of Prophets. Both Hassan and Hussain squalled in anguish: "O grandfather! O Messenger of Allah!" Whilst Fatimah al-Zahra called out: "O father! O my Muhammad! O beloved!" Then she fell unconscious.

The Commander of the Faithfuls (peace be upon him), lifted the holy body of the Prophet and prepared it for the wash. Salman al-Muhammadi [al-Farisi] narrates: "I went to Ali when he was performing the Ghusl (i.e. funeral wash) for the Messenger of Allah (peace be upon him and his family). The Messenger had instructed by will that only Ali performs the wash for him and informed that whenever Ali would need to turn a part of his body over, the part would be turned over to him [on its own by the will of Allah]" Salman continues: "The Commander of the Faithfuls had asked the Prophet

---

[8] Al-Irshad by al-Mufid

who would help me perform the wash for you O Messenger of Allah? The Prophet said: Gabriel."

When the holy body of the Prophet (peace be upon him and his family) was washed and draped in a shroud, Ali (peace be upon him) allowed Salman, Abu Dhar, Miqdad, Fatimah, Hassan and Hussain in; They aligned behind him, and he led them in the funeral prayer. Aisha was in the [same] chamber but she did not know [what was happening] as Gabriel took away her sight. Then angels came in crowds; they stood behind The Commander of the Faithfuls (peace be upon him) and were led by him to perform the funeral prayer.

When people became aware of the Prophet's death, Madinah was grief-stricken; loud cries and weeping were heard. The Muhajireen and Ansar came in crowds to the house of the Prophet (peace be upon him and his family). Ten of each group were allowed into the chamber at a time by the Commander of the Faithfuls (peace be upon him) to offer prayers upon the Prophet; A group would leave and another one would enter successively, so that no one remains from the Muhajireen or Ansar but to have invoked prayers on him. [9]

When Umar ibn al-Khattab (may the wrath of Allah be upon him) saw the crowds flocking to the house of the Prophet, at the time when Abu Bakr was in

____

[9] Kitab Sulaim ibn Qays

Sunh in the suburb of Madinah, he feared they would pledge their allegiance to Ali ibn Abi Talib (peace be upon him), the Prophet's legitimate successor and thus his desire and the desire of Abu Bakr to lead the caliphate is never fulfilled, so he sought diligently to hinder this from happening at every turn. He drew his sword out of its sheath roaming the alleyways of Madinah terrorising and deceiving people by saying: "Allah's Messenger did not die, nor will he die until his religion reigns over all other religions. He shall return to amputate the hands and legs of the men who spread rumours about his death.[10]

"Hypocrites allege that the Messenger of Allah has died. By Allah, he has not died but rather he has gone to his Lord just as Moses son of Imran did; He remained in occultation away from his people for forty nights after which he returned to them. By Allah, the Messenger of Allah shall return and shall amputate the hands and legs of those who claim that he died[11]. I will not hear a man say: `The Messenger of Allah died', save that I will strike him with my sword."[12]

Umar sent Salim ibn Ubaid to Abu Bakr to inform him about the death of the Messenger of Allah and about the importance of his immediate return to Madinah so that the opportunity to take over the

---

[10] Sharh al-Nahj by Ibn abi al-Hadid
[11] Al-Sirah al-Nabawiyah by Ibn Hisham
[12] Sharh al-Nahj by ibn abi al-Hadid

caliphate is not wasted! Abu Bakr then hastened down to Madinah. When Umar saw Abu Bakr, he showed calmness although he was just swearing that the Messenger of Allah did not die. Abu Bakr said: "O oath-taker! Don't be hasty! Whoever worshipped Muhammad, then Muhammad is dead, but whoever worshipped Allah, then Allah is alive and shall never die."[13]

Suddenly, Umar's frantic tone calmed down and he gave the expression as if he had woken up from a frenzy of rage. However, in reality Umar deceptively pretended to be so much emotionally stricken with the crowning aim to suspend the Muslims and hinder the *Bay'a*, oath of allegiance, to Ali (peace be upon him) until the arrival of Abu Bakr so that he can deceivingly act upon his premeditated plan to seize the caliphate.

While the pure household of the Prophet were afflicted by the tragic death of the Messenger of Allah and stricken by the irremediable catastrophe of his loss, consoling and solacing one another, the hypocrites Abu Barkr and Umar were eagerly aiming for leadership and busy working to achieve this aim. They did not attend the funeral of the holy Prophet, nor did they offer the funeral prayer on his body but rather they rushed to the Saqifah of Bani Sa'idah especially after knowing that the Ansar were assembling there to endorse the caliph to be.

---

[13] Sahih al-Bukhari vol. 03 H. 3467

Intense dissension arose between the two parties; Each threatening and cursing the other. It was said: "There should be one 'Amir from us and one from you", until Umar managed to wangle the caliphate to be delegated to Abu Bakr son of Abu Quhafah.[14]

The Prophet's uncle, al-Abbas, came to the Commander of the Faithfuls (peace be upon him) and said: "O Ali! Stretch out your hand let me pledge allegiance to you, so that [people] say the Messenger's uncle gave his allegiance to the Messenger's cousin, then your household give their allegiance to you too; If this happens the matter will not seem of little significance."

Ali (peace be upon him) refused and said: "Who is after this matter apart from us?"[15] Whilst they were speaking, they suddenly heard people's acclamation in the mosque of the holy Prophet of Allah chanting: "Allah is the Greatest, there is no God but Allah". They [saw] Abu Bakr surrounded by Umar and Ubaida ibn al-Jarrah while all the other people took him in a procession like that of a bride on her wedding day towards the pulpit to announce the beginning of his leadership. Ali (peace be upon him) said bewilderingly: "What is this?!", al-Abbas replied: "The like of this has never been seen before, did I not tell you!?"[16]

---

14 Sahih al-Bukhari vol. 3 H. 3467
15 Al-Imamah wal Siyasah by Ibn Qutaiba
16 Al-Iqd al-Farid, vol. 04

Fatimah wailed: "Alas, what a bad morning." Abu Bakr heard this and said, "Your morning is bad[17], [Your bad days have arrived]. Some people's disasters are other's benefits".[18]

Some of the Prophet's companions, who were present at the Prophet's Mosque at the time became angry at Abu Bakr's seizure of leadership and the allegiance he was given by the Muslims. This is because they had given their allegiance to the Commander of the Faithfuls at Ghadeer Khum by the order of the Prophet (peace be upon him and his family).

Therefore, Salman, Miqdad, Abu Dhar, Zubair, Talha, al-Abbas and a group of Bani Hashim proceeded towards Ali's house. Umar headed there too with a group of men who had pledged their allegiance to Abu Bakr, amongst whom were Usaid ibn Hudair and Salama ibn Salamah. When he arrived there, he so them all gathered. Umar said: "Give your allegiance to Abu Bakr for people have already given their allegiance to him"! Zubair leaped and drew his sword out. Umar said: "Get hold of this dog! Drive away his evil!" Salama ibn Salamah snatched the sword away from Zaubair's hand. Umar took the sword, struck it against the ground and broke it. Then they turned to the group of men from Bani Hashim

---

17 Al-Irshad by al-Mufis
18 Mathalib al-Nawasib by Ibn Shahr Aashub, vol. 3

and surrounded them and went along with The Commander of the Faithfuls (peace be upon him) to Abu Bakr. [Upon arrival] they were told: "Pledge allegiance to Abu Bakr for people have already given their allegiance to him! By Allah if you refuse, we shall raise our swords against you!".

Upon hearing this, one by one started to give their allegiance to Abu Bakr until no one remained of those present apart from Ali (peace be upon him).

Ali (peace be upon him) was told: "give the oath of allegiance to Abu Bakr!" Ali (peace be upon him) said: "I am more deserving of this position than him, and it is incumbent on you to pledge allegiance to me. You have taken this right from the Ansar based on your relationship with the Messenger of Allah (peace be upon him and his family) while you seize it away from us and we are his immediate household!? Did you not take the matter away from the Ansar claiming that you are more deserving than them of it based on your close relationship and thus they gave up the leadership to you. I also argue on the same ground; I am more deserving of this position in the life of the Messenger and after his death. I am his successor and heir; I am the store of his knowledge and secrets. I am the greatest to be known for his truthfulness (i.e. *al-Sidiqq al-Akbar*); The first to believe the Prophet and the first to believe in him.

"I am the one with the distinguishing performance in the wars with non-believers out of all of you. I am the most knowing of the Quran and Sunnah, the most versed in the religion and the most knowledgeable of the outcome of all affairs. Out of all of you, I am the one with the sharpest tongue; The one with the most resolute [unshakeable] heart. For what reason do you quarrel me over this matter?! Be just, if you fear Allah, and accept that this is our right just how the Ansar accepted it be a right of yours. Otherwise [if you refuse to accept] then incur [the outcome of your] intentional oppression while you are fully aware of it".

He then addressed the Muhajireen and Ansar by saying: "O company of Muhajireen and Ansar, fear Allah! Do not forget the oath you have given to your Prophet with regards to my [guardianship]. Do not take away the authority of Muhammad from his house and the inside of his home to your houses and the inside of your homes! [Do not] drive away his family from his right and position within people.

"O congregations! Allah had ordained and adjudged the [authority of us AhlulBayt] and his Messenger declared it and thus you know it. We the AhlulBayt have greater authority of this matter than you. Is it not from us [the AhlulBayt] the most versed in the book of Allah; The [most] knowledgeable of the religion of Allah; The most informed about the matters and affairs of people? By Allah, we have [these virtues] and not you. Refrain from following your own desire for [if you do so] you will distance yourselves further away from the truth and ruin your old [good deeds] with your evil late [ones]".

Umar said: "Would you not take [Bani Hashim] an example, [follow what they did and give your allegiance]?" To which Ali (peace be upon him] replied: "Ask them about it".

The men from Bani Hashim who paid the allegiance then rushed and said: "Our allegiance [to Abu Bakr] is not an argument against Ali. We seek Allah's refuge from claiming that we are equivalent to him with regards to his migration and well performance in battlefields [striving in the cause of Allah] or to his position to the Messenger of Allah".

Umar said to Ali (peace be upon him): "You will not be left until you give your allegiance willingly or by the use of coercion. Ali (peace be upon him) said: "Milk some milk so that you can [benefit] and have a portion of it. You insist upon it today So that you can take it tomorrow. By Allah, I will not heed your command and will not care about your position; And I shall not pledge allegiance to him."

Bashir ibn Sa'd al-Ansari, who was amongst the people who gave allegiance to Abu Bakr, along with a group of men from the Ansar, said: "O Abal Hassan! Had the Ansar heard your words before joining Abu Bakr, no one would have disagreed about you! Ali (peace be upon him) said: "O you! would you expect me to leave the Messenger of Allah shrouded and not bury him and come out to challenge on the matter [of Caliphate]?! [Certainly] you had pledged allegiance to me [on Ghadeer Khum] before you gave allegiance to Abu Bakr, in the presence of the Messenger and Allah had ordained it beforehand. Did the two of them not pledge their allegiance to me? Then why do they claim something that is neither theirs nor they are worthy of it?!

"By Allah, I was not afraid that one would argue us the household of the Prophet [about the matter of successorship] and deem it permissible to take it away the same way you are doing, [since] the Messenger of Allah (peace be upon him and his family) had left no one uninformed on the day of Ghadeer Khum about the matter as the conclusive proof was fully established. By Allah, I appeal to anyone of you, who had heard the Prophet (peace be upon him and his family) say: 'Of whomsoever I am a master, Ali is his master. My Lord! Befriend anyone who befriends him and make enmity towards anyone who makes enmity towards him and help anyone who helps him and leave alone anyone who leaves him alone' to bear witness [now] of what he heard."

Zaid ibn Arqam said: "Twelve men amongst those who were present at the battle of Badr testified that they had heard the Prophet saying it. However, although I was [also] one of the ones who had heard the saying from the Prophet, I did not give my testimony on that day and [as a result of this misdeed] I lost my eyesight."

There was a great deal of speaking, and the voices were raising. Umar feared that people would listen to what Ali (peace be upon him) was saying and thus he adjourned the assembly and said: "Allah turns hearts and eyes over" Then everyone left on that day".[19]

Fulfilling the will of the Messenger of Allah (peace be upon him and his family), the Commander of the Faithfuls then secluded himself from the people and confined himself to his house and set about to compile and arrange the Quran. There was a great deal of talk by the people about his refusal to pledge allegiance to Abu Bakr. People started to lay the blame on each other for deserting him as the legitimate successor of the Messenger of Allah and supporting Abu Bakr instead. As a result, some people refused to pledge allegiance to Abu Bakr. This made Abu Bakr and Umar very aggravated. Umar sought the help of A'rab and *Ajlaf*, gruff and ill-natured group of men, to compel people to give allegiance to Abu Bakr.

---

[19] Bihar al-Anwar vol. 28

Said Za'idatu Ibnu Qudamah: "A group of ill-natured A'rab entered Madinah to gather food. People were preoccupied with the death of the Messenger of Allah and therefore the A'rab witnessed the pledge of allegiance to Abu Bakr. Umar then summoned them and said: 'Head out to the people, gather them, and force them to give allegiance. Should one refuse, hit him on his face and forehead'" Za'idah continued: "By Allah, I saw the A'rab buckling their belts, wrapping themselves with [Yemeni] Sanaa coverings, picking up woods in their hands and then they headed out badly beating and coercing [people] to give allegiance."[20]

Some of the Muhajireen and Ansar flocked to the Prophet's house and said to Ali (peace be upon him): "By Allah, you are the Commander of the Faithfuls; You are by Allah the most rightful person and the one who has the strongest affinity to the Prophet. Put forth your hand so that we can pledge allegiance to you, for by Allah we are going to die in front of you in your defence.[21] By Allah, we shall not be obedient to anyone but you". Ali (peace be upon him) said: "And why?" They said: "Verily, we heard the Messenger of Allah's speech about you on the Day of Ghadeer". Ali said: "Would you act by it?". They said: "Yes"! Ali (peace be upon him) said: "If you are truthful then come to me tomorrow

---

[20] Al-Jamal by al-Mufid
[21] Bihar al-Anwar vol. 22

having shaved your head" No one came [the next day] to him apart from Salman, Miqdad, Abu Dhar and some say Zubair as well. However, Ammar came past midday! When The Commander of the Faithfuls saw only a few came on, he said to them: "Go back for I have no need of you. You did not obey me in the shaving of the head so how would you obey me in fighting the mountains of iron"!?[22]

Umar then came to Abu Bakr and told him: "Are you not going to take him (i.e. he means Ali peace be upon him) for refusing to give allegiance to you?[23] All people have given their allegiance to you apart from this man, his household and this group.[24] Send to Ali to pay allegiance for there is no value in this [caliphate] until he pays allegiance.[25] O you, there is nothing in your hands if Ali does not pledge his allegiance to you therefore send for him to come and pledge his allegiance to you so that these people can see it"[26]

Abu Bakr then sent Qunfudh to Ali (peace be upon him) and told him: "Go and tell Ali to answer the vicegerent of Allah's Messenger" Qunfudh went and soon came back and told Abu Bakr: "He said: by Allah, the Messenger of Allah (peace be upon him and his family) has not appointed anyone but myself. How fast have you attributed a lie to the

---

22 Bihar al-Anwar vol.28 and al-Ikhtisas by al-Mufid
23 Al-Imamah wal Siyasah by ibn Qutaibah
24 Kitab Sulaim ibn Qays
25 Bihar al-Anwar vol. 28
26 Tafsir al-Ayashi vol. 2

Messenger of Allah (peace be upon him and his family) and reverted [to disbelief]. O Qunfudh tell Abu Bakr, verily you know who the vicegerent of Allah's Messenger is" Abu Bakr said: "Ali has spoken the truth. The Messenger of Allah did not appoint me to be his vicegerent"

Umar then said: "O Qunfudh, return back and tell him the Muslims' appointed caliph is calling you". Qunfudh returned to Ali (peace be upon him) and conveyed the message. Ali (peace be upon him) said: "He who has been appointed is verily inferior to the one who appointed him, and the appointee has no authority to command the one who appointed him"![27]

When Qunfudh returned back and delivered Ali's message, Umar became ferocious; He leapt up and said to Abu Bakr: "Are you not going to get this [man] who has refused to pay allegiance to you in your grip?! Abu Bakr said: "Sit down" Then he said to Qunfudh: "Go back [to Ali] and tell him answer The Commander of the Faithfuls Abu Bakr"!

Qunfudh returned to Ali (peace be upon him) and conveyed the message. Ali (peace be upon him) said: "By Allah, he has told a lie! Go back and tell him you have given yourself a title that is not for you. You know that The Commander of the Faithfuls is not you. Glory be to Allah! By Allah, it has not been long

---

[27] Al-Kashkool by Sayed Haidar al-Aamuli

so that he forgets. By Allah, he knows that no one is worthy of this title but myself. Verily, he was commanded by the Messenger of Allah (peace be upon him and his family) - and he was the seventh in number - to salute me as The Commander of the Faithfuls". Qunfudh then went back to Abu Bakr and Umar and conveyed the message.[28]

Umar leapt up vexedly and said: "By Allah, I know his absurdity and the weakness of his opinion. This caliphate cannot be right for us until we do kill him. You leave me, I will bring his head." Abu Bakr said: "Sit down" He refused, so Abu Bakr held him under oath, so he sat down and said: "O Qunfudh, go and tell him answer Abu Bakr [for he is calling you]".

Qunfudh came and said: "O Ali, Abu Bakr is calling you." Ali (peace be upon him) said: "I am too occupied to answer him! I am not the one to leave the will of my brother and friend and instead go to Abu Bakr and [see] the despotism you have united on. The Messenger of Allah told and commanded me by will that once I bury him in his grave, I must not leave my house before compiling the book of Allah for it is [written] on the leafstalks of date palms and the scapula of camels".

Then they kept silent for some days, during which Ali (peace be upon him) managed to compile the Quran [from start to end] in a single garment. He

---

[28] Kitab Sulaim ibn Qais

then went out to the people, who were gathered around Abu Bakr in the mosque of the Holy Prophet (peace be upon him and his family) and declared loudly: "O people! From the moment of the Messenger's departure, I have been busy with giving him the funeral wash and then with the Quran until I compiled it all in this single garment. There is not a verse revealed upon the Messenger, which I have not collected, and there is not a verse revealed, which the Messenger did not recite it to me and taught me its meaning. This is lest you might say tomorrow 'We were not aware of this'. This is lest you might say on the Day of Judgement I had not called you to support me; I had not reminded you of my right and had not called you to the Book of Allah from its beginning to its end.[29]

Umar said tauntingly: "What you have with you is of no use to us at all, because of what we have with us from the Quran" Ali (peace be upon him) then isolated himself away from the people in his house.

At night Ali (peace be upon him) carried Fatimah (peace be upon her) on a mounting animal and held the hands of his two sons Hassan and Hussain (peace be upon them) and there was no single companion of the Holy Prophet (peace be upon him and his pure family) left to whose house he did not go, and whom Zahra did not urge by Allah of Ali's rights and called them to help him.

---

[29] Kitab Sulaim ibn Qays

The companions said to Fatimah: "O daughter of the Messenger! We have already given our allegiance to that man [i.e. Abu bakr]. Had your spouse come to us first before Abu Bakr, we would not have chosen anyone but him!" To which The Commander of the Faithfuls (peace be upon him) replied: "Did you expect me to leave the [body] of the Messenger of Allah in his house unburied and go out to challenge the people on the matter of successorship? Fatimah (peace be upon her) said: "*Abul Hassan* [The father of Hassan i.e Ali peace be upon him] did what he should have done, but they did what Allah will judge and call them to account for".[30]

No man answered Ali's call for support except for four; They shaved their heads and offered him full support. When Ali (peace be upon him) saw people's failure to support him and their general consensus on Abu Bakr, he confined himself to his house again.[31]

After a few days passed, Umar said to Abu Bakr: "What is stopping you to send someone to [force him] to pledge allegiance?"[32] And if you do not do so I will!" He then went out and started calling out the different tribes and clans irefully: "Answer the Caliph"! People then answered him from every

---

[30] Al-Imamah Wal Siyasah by Ibn Qutaybah
[31] Kitab Sulaim ibn Qays, and Bihar al-Anwar vol. 28
[32] Kitab Sulaim ibn Qays

place and corner until a total of three hundred crime syndicates gathered around him. He then made them enter upon Abu Bakr and said: "I have gathered for you the men and horses".[33]

Amongst those men were: Uthman ibn Affan, Khalid ibn al-Walid, Abdul-Rahman ibn Aouf, Abu Ubaidah ibn al-Jarrah, Salim the slave of Abi Hudhaifah, Qunfudh Umar's cousin, Usaid ibn Hudhair, Salamah ibnu Salamah and Hurmus al-Farisi.

Abu Bakr said to Umar: "Who shall we send to him" Umar said: "[This should be] Qunfudh, for he is rough, hard-hearted and brutal, send him along with other men to aid him"[34] He added: "Force them to leave the house. Should they resist, then collect wood at his door and warn them if they refuse to give their allegiance you will set the house on fire"[35]

Qunfudh headed to Ali's house and asked permission to enter, but Ali did not grant him permission. Qunfudh's companions went back to Abu Bakr and Umar, who were in the mosque surrounded by other men, and said: "We were not given permission". Umar said: "Head there [again], either he allows you in or you enter without permission" They headed there and asked for permission. Fatimah (peace be upon her) said: "I forbid you from entering my house without my

---

33 Al-Kawkabul Duriy by al-Masindarani
34 Bihar al-Anwar, vol. 28
35 Al-Jamal by al-Mufid

permission" While Qunfudh remained, his companions returned back and said: "Fatimah said so and so, thus we avoided entering her house without permission"[36]

Upon hearing this Umar was enraged[37]; He leaped up and said angrily: "What do we have to do with women"!? Then he called Qunfudh and Khalid ibn al-Walid and ordered them to take some wood and fire.[38] Abu Bakr said: "Bring him to me in the most violent way[39]; Drive them out and if they refuse then fight them![40]

Then they brought along wood and fire[41], and Umar came with a wick of fire[42]. He shouted: "If they refuse to come out to pledge allegiance, I shall burn the house down upon them![43] Someone said: "Fatimah and both Hassan and Hussain are inside the house! Umar said: "So what! [Let them be]". Then they spearheaded to Ali's house intent on burning the house down with everyone in it.

Narrates Ubay ibnu Ka'b: "We heard the neighing of steeds, rattling of reins and the clattering of spearheads, so we went out of our houses in our garments and joined the people until they got to

---

36 Al-Ihtijaj by al-Tabarsi
37 Majma' al-Zawaid and Kanz al-Ummal
38 Kitab Sulaim ibn Qays
39 Ansab al-Ashraf by al-Balatheri vol. 5
40 Al-Iqd al-Farid by ibn Abd Rabih vol. 5
41 Kitab Sulaim ibn Qays
42 Ansab al-Ashraf by al-Balathiri
43 Al-Shafi by ibn Hamza

Ali's house"[44] Fatimah (peace be upon her) was sitting behind the door and she had a strip tied to her head, and her body had become very weak due to the demise of the Holy Prophet (peace be upon him and his family)[45] Once she saw them she closed the door. She had no doubt that they would not enter her house but with her permission.[46]

They banged the door vigorously[47], raised their voices and addressed those who were inside the house with different speeches[48] and called on them to pledge allegiance to Abu Bakr.[49]

Umar shouted loudly: "O son of Abu Talib, open the door.[50] By Allah, if you do not open the door, we shall burn it down with fire.[51] By Him in whose hands is my soul you either come out to pledge allegiance or I will burn the house down upon you.[52] O Ali! You either come out [to agree] on what Muslims have all agreed on, or we will kill you![53] O son of Abu Talib, if you do not come out and enter wholeheartedly into what people have entered into, I will burn the house down upon whomever is in it.[54] O son of Abu Talib, you either open the door, or I will burn your house

---

[44] Al-Kawkab al-Durri by al-Mazindarani
[45] Kitab Sulaim ibn Qays
[46] Tafsir al-Ayashi vol. 2
[47] Dala'il al-Imamah by al-Tabari vol. 2
[48] Hadiqatul Shia
[49] Al-Shafi by ibn Hamza
[50] Kitab Sulaim ibn Qays
[51] Ilm al-Yaqin vol. 2
[52] Al-Saqifah by al-Jawhari
[53] Bihar al-Anwar vol.53
[54] Al-Kashkool

upon you![55] By Allah, you either come out to pledge allegiance to the Messenger's successor, or I will set fire to you. O Ali, you either come out, or I will burn the house down."[56]

Fatimah then stood behind the door and said: "O you astray, the beliers, what are you saying and what is it that you want?" Umar said: "O Fatimah!" She replied: "What do you want Umar?" Umar said: "What is it with your spouse? He made you answer while he sat behind the veil?" Fatimah said: "It is your tyranny, you wretched, that made me come out, so that proof is established upon you and upon every astray and deviant one."

Umar said: "Leave your falsehood behind and the fables [nonsense] of women and tell Ali to come out" Fatimah (peace be upon her) said: "To my displeasure! Are you threatening me with the party of Satan, O Umar? Verily, the party of Satan is weak." Umar said: "Either he comes out [now] or I will bring plenty of wood and set this house on fire, burning everyone in it, or rather Ali shall be dragged by force to pledge allegiance!"[57] Fatimah (peace be upon her) said: "O Umar, what have you got to do with us? Would you not leave us alone?" Umar said: "You either open the door, or we shall set your house on fire![58] O Fatimah! Bring out all of those sitting in your

---

55 Kamil al-Baha'ie by Imad al-Din al-Tabari
56 Kitab Sulaim ibn Qays
57 Dala'il al-Imamah by al-Tabari
58 Kitab Sulaim ibn Qays

house to pledge allegiance and enter into what all Muslims have entered into, or I shall burn them all with fire.[59] Enter into what the Ummah has entered into![60]

"O Fatimah! Get whoever is congregating inside to come out, or I will burn this house down!"[61] Fatimah (peace be upon her) said: "Are you going to burn my children?" Umar said: "By Allah, indeed I will, or you get them to come out and pledge their allegiance."[62] Fatimah said: "O son of Abul Khattab, are you going to burn my door down upon me?" Umar said: "Indeed!"[63]

Fatimah (peace be upon her) said; "Woe be to you O Umar! You have the audacity [and transgression] before Allah and his Messenger!? You intend to cut off his offspring in this life and extinguish the light of Allah while Allah intends to perfect his light!?" Umar said: "Stop it O Fatimah for neither Muhammad is present, nor the angels are coming down with the commands, prohibitions and reprimands of Allah! Ali is no one but a mere Muslim, so it is your choice either to get him out to pledge allegiance to Abu Bakr, or you may wish to be all burnt!"

Fatimah wailed: "O Allah, to You we complain the loss of Your Prophet, Your Messenger and Your

---

[59] Al-Jamal by al-Mufid
[60] Rawdatul Nadhir
[61] Kamil al-Baha'ie by Imad al-Din al-Tabari
[62] Al-Tara'if
[63] Ansab al-Ashraf by Al-Balathiri vol. 01

chosen one. [We complain to You] his Ummah, turning against us and seizing us of the rights that you have given to us and stated for us in Your book that was sent down to Your Prophet." Umar said: "O Fatimah! Spare yourself the foolishness of women, Allah is not going to give you both, Prophethood and successorship!"[64] Fatimah (peace be upon her said: "O Umar! Would you not fear Allah, you dare to trespass and attack my house!?" Despite this, Umar (may the wrath of Allah be upon him) refused to go away.[65]

Umar then ordered for wood to be put all around the house, and he held a wick of fire in his hands.[66] He started shouting: "Burn her house down with whomever is in it."[67]

Fatimah (peace be upon her) then cried at the top of her voice: "O father, O Messenger of Allah! What have the sons of al-Khattab, and Abu Quhafah done to us after you! When people heard her voice they walked away in tears, while Umar remained with a group of people.[68]

Qunfudh then reached in, aiming to open the door.[69] Fatimah held onto the doorposts, trying to stop them from breaking in and said: "I implore you

---

64 Bihar al-Anwar vol. 53
65 Kitab Sulaim ibn Qays
66 Tafsir al-Ayashi vol. 02
67 Al-Milal wal Nihal by al-Shihristani
68 Al-Imamah wal Siyasah by Ibn Qutaibah vol. 01
69 Bihar al-Anwar vol. 53

for the sake of Allah and my father the Messenger of Allah to leave us alone and go away!" Umar then called for the fire and ignited the door[70], and thus the door was in flames[71], and the smoke entered the house.[72]

Umar pushed the door open with his foot, so the door broke down. He then broke into the house with the scoundrels who were with him. Fatimah (peace be upon her) was behind the door wailing. Umar coerced Fatimah into holding onto the doorpost and then he (may the wrath of Allah be upon him) crushed her violently and with full force between the door and the wall; Fatimah's soul was almost going to be torn from her body.

As a result, Fatimah's rib was broken and due to the crunch the door nail pierced into Fatimah's chest and the blood gushed forth. Umar then, slapped Fatimah (peace be upon her) on her cheek and caused her eye to become red and her earrings to tear and scatter on the ground in bits. Umar then kicked Fatimah (peace be upon her), lifted his sword as it was inside its sheath and struck her side with it and raised the whip and lathered her arm and again her wrist. The whip twisted itself around Fatimah's wrists, leaving a mark like a black

---

[70] Kitab Sulaim ibn Qays
[71] Bihar al-Anwar vol. 53
[72] Al-Shafi by al-Sayed al-Murtadha

bracelet [73]. Umar continued to hit her on her shoulder.

Al-Mughira ibn Shu'bah then hit Fatimah (peace be upon her) so violently and caused her to bleed. Then Khalid ibn al-Walid pulled a sword out of its sheath to hit Fatimah, whilst Qunfudh raised the back of his sword and with full force hit Fatimah with it. Qunfudh then raised his whip and lathered her back and side until she felt strained. Then Umar kicked Fatimah (peace be upon her) again with his foot in her stomach, due to which Fatimah collapsed to the floor and miscarried her foetus, named al-Muhassin[74].

Fatimah (peace be upon her) then screamed out of agony and wailed: "O father! O Messenger of Allah! This is what they have done to your beloved daughter".

She then groaned: "O Fiddah! To you take me for the accursed have killed the [baby] inside of me".[75] The Commander of the Faithfuls (peace be upon him) then came out of the house red-eyed and bare-headed; He casted his mantle on her and embraced her to his chest and squalled: "O Fiddah! [Rush to] Your mistress! Tend to her as women are

---

[73] Bihar al-Anwar vol. 53
[74] Al-Hidayah al-Kubra
[75] Bihar al-Anwar vol. 30

tended to for she is experiencing the pain of childbirth due to the kick".[76]

Ali (peace be upon him) then leaped up and grabbed Umar by his lapels; He shook him then struck him down and clouted his nose and neck intending to kill him, but he remembered that the Messenger of Allah (peace be upon him and his pure family) had enjoined him to remain dutiful and patient so he said: "O son of Suhak! By The One Who honoured Muhammad (peace be upon him and his family) with prophethood, had I not been entrusted with the divine order and the will of the Messenger of Allah, you would know that you had no power to enter my house".

Umar then started calling for help whilst under the feet of The Commander of the Faithfuls, upon which people started coming into the house. Qunfudh then returned to Abu Bakr as he was fearing that Ali (peace be upon him) might come out wielding his sword since he knew he was a man of courage and valour. Upon his return Abu Bakr said: "Go back, he either comes out or you break into the house [and force him to come out]. Should he refuse, then set the house on fire!" Qunfudh then returned with his people and broke into The Commander of the Faithful's house.

---

[76] Bihar al-Anwar vol. 53

Ali (peace be upon him) then rushed to grab his sword, but the people, who were of a significant number, preceded to it before him and surrounded him[77]. Ali (peace be upon him) committed to the will of the Messenger of Allah to abide by patience, and thus he did not resist them.

They eventually managed to [get hold of him] and tie a rope in his neck[78]. They dragged him outside the house pulling the upper part of his clothes and headed towards the Prophet's mosque. At that time, Fatimah (peace be upon her) [barely] managed to pull herself together and tried to intercept between them and cried: "By Allah, I will not allow you to drag my spouse unjustly. May woe be unto you! How swiftly have you sought to betray Allah and His Messenger by [mistreating us], the household"[79].

The Commander of the Faithfuls (peace be upon him) was then dragged by force outside his house and driven violently to the mosque like a tethered camel[80], amidst wielded swords. He was indignant and raging from within but yet very patient and very restraining of his desperate anger. He was brought into the mosque exhausted, while people congregated observing as the alleyways of Madinah were thronged with men.

---

[77] Kitab Sulaim ibn Qays
[78] Kitab Sulaim Ibn Qays
[79] Al-Kawkabul Durri by al-Mazindarani
[80] Waq'at Sifin by Nasr ibn Muzahim

Salman, Abu Dhar, Miqdad, Ammar and Buraidah followed the Commander of the Faithfuls (peace be upon him) crying through the way: "How swiftly have you betrayed the Messenger of Allah and gotten the grudges off your chests. Buraida ibnul Husaib al-Aslami then stood up and said to Umar: "O Umar! You have attacked the brother of the Messenger of Allah, who is his successor and you have beaten his daughter, and you are that very person whose [disreputable] reputation is very well known in Quraysh, O son of Suhak!"[81]

As the Commander of the Faithfuls (peace be upon him) was in agony, he said: "By Allah, had I had my sword in my hand, you would have known that you would not be at all able to attain this. By Allah! I would not have blamed myself, if I had to fight against you. Had I had forty [supporting] men, I would verily have dispersed those who have rallied behind you but may the curse of Allah be upon those who had pledged their allegiance to me and then betrayed me.[82] Oh Jaffar, and there is no Jaffar for me today! Oh Hamza, and there is no Hamza for me today."[83]

The Commander of the Faithfuls (peace be upon him) was then passed by the grave of the holy Prophet (peace be upon him and his family); He stopped there and said: "O son of my mother! Lo,

---

81 Kitab Sulaim ibn Qays
82 Kitab Sulaim ibn Qays
83 Sharh al-Nahj by Ibn Abi al-Hadid vol.11

the people oppressed me and were about to kill me!" Immediately a hand was seen stretched out of the Messenger's grave, they knew it was the Messenger's hand, and a voice was heard, they knew it was his voice towards Abu Bakr: "O you! Have you disbelieved in He Who created you from soil, then from a drop, and then proportioned you as a man?"[84]

When Salman witnessed this, he said: "Does this happen to [him]? By Allah, if he was to plead Allah earnestly, certainly the heavens would fall, and the earth would rend"[85] While Abu Dhar said: "If only we get our swords in our hands again!"[86]

Fatimah (peace be upon her) then came out having the shirt of the Messenger of Allah on her head and holding the hands of both of her sons crying and wailing. However, people were telling her to stop what she was doing.

At that time, all Hashimi women came out to accompany her. Fatimah cried, wailed and called out: "O Abu Bakr! How swiftly have you assailed the household of the Messenger of Allah? By Allah, I shall not speak to Umar until I meet my Lord.[87] Leave my spouse. O Abu Bakr! What do you have to do with

---

[84] Basa'ir al-Darajat
[85] Al-Ikhtisas by al-Mufid
[86] Rijal al-Kashi
[87] Sharh al-Nahj by ibn Abi al-Hadid vol. 02

me? Do you want to orphan my two sons and widow me?

"Surely if you do not leave him alone, I shall dishevel my hair, tear my collars, and head to the grave of my father imploring my Lord, for Salih [the Prophet] is verily not more honoured by Allah than my spouse, neither the camel of Salih is more honoured by Allah than I am, nor the calf is more honoured than my children."

Ali (peace be upon him) said to Salman: "Rush to the daughter of Muhammad for I can see the two sides of Madinah falling in! By Allah, if she was to dishevel her hair, tear her collars, head to the grave of her father and complain to her Lord, [Allah will cause] Madinah and wherever is in it to sink into the earth."

Narrates Salman (peace be upon him): "By Allah! I witnessed the base of the columns of the mosque uprooting; If a man wanted to pass through it, he would be able to![88] So I rushed to her and said: "O daughter of Muhammad, Allah has sent your father as a mercy, so [I beseech you] to go back!"

Fatimah (peace be upon her) said: "O Salman! They want to kill Ali, and therefore I cannot stay patient." Salman said: "O my Grace and Mistress, I fear that Madinah will sink into the earth [as a punishment for them]; Verily Ali (peace be upon him) sent me to you

---

[88] Al-Mustarshid by al-Tabari

and he is asking you to go back home" Fatimah (peace be upon her) said: "I shall indeed go back then, practice patience, listen to him and obey."[89]

Salman narrates: "Only then the columns of the mosque rested on the grounds again, blowing dust from underneath into our noses."[90]

Fatimah (peace be upon her) then turned to the grave of her father (peace be upon him and his pure family), beckoning to it and poeticising in grief:

My soul is confined by its deep sighs
I wish it is breathed out with the sighs

Verily there is no good in living after you
I only cry fearing of a prolonged life after you

Then she said: "O father! How grieved I am about you! How bereaved is your trusted one and beloved, Abu al-Hassan; The father of your two grandsons, Hassan and Hussain; The one whom you brought up and cared for when he was young, and with whom you instituted brotherhood when he was older; The most esteemed and the most loved by you out of all your companions; The first to embrace to Islam and the first to migrate to you! O the best of all creation, here he is driven into captivity like a [fleeting] camel!"

---

[89] Tafsir al-Ayashi vol. 02
[90] Al-Mustarshid by al-Tabari

She (peace be upon her) then groaned and said: "Oh Muhammad! Oh beloved! Oh father! Oh father of Qasim! Oh Ahmad! Alas, there aren't enough supporters! Alas, a cry for help! Alas, long is my distress! Alas, how grieved I am! Alas, how afflicted I am! Alas, what a bad morning!"

Due to being traumatised, Fatimah (peace be upon her) collapsed and became unconscious and people started wailing and mourning in the mosque.[91]

------

[91] Ilm al-Yaqin